WILD
WEATHER

CAROLINE HARRIS

QUOTATIONS AND FOREWORD BY
WARREN FAIDLEY

KINGFISHER

WELCOME TO THE VOYAGE

Storm chaser
Warren Faidley has been chasing storms for more than 20 years. He is a photographer who takes amazing pictures of extreme weather, and has become an expert on storm behaviour.

Dear Voyager,
My name is Warren Faidley and I will be your storm chaser guide as you journey through this book. In the next pages we look at what shapes the Earth's weather. Then, in chapter one, we will experience the full force of water, from incredible clouds to devastating floods. In chapter two, we track awe-inspiring storms, including hurricanes and tornadoes. Finally, we travel through extremes of heat and cold. As you explore the book, you will find extra features to help you on your way. You can turn the transparent pages to see an amazing lightning show or the path of a twister, and unfold the dramatic story of a drought. And you can read my quotations to learn about my own experiences of wild weather.

The power of the elements
From floods to wildfires and dust storms to avalanches, wild weather takes many different forms. Extreme weather can also cause terrible damage and loss of life.

On the trail
Storm chasing can be dangerous, especially if you do not know what you are doing. Warren is very careful about safety. His storm chasing truck even has extra-tough glass to guard against hail.

A storm chaser is someone who tracks down wild weather in order to study, photograph or simply experience it. Some chasers are scientists who want to learn about what happens inside a storm. Others help to predict or spot where a tornado is forming so that the people who live nearby can be warned in time. The United States has a lot of the world's wildest weather. With my storm-chasing truck, maps and forecasting equipment, I travel to different parts of the country to capture these events on my camera. In the spring, I go on the trail of tornadoes in the Great Plains, and later I catch thunderstorms in the desert around where I live, in Tucson, Arizona. In the late summer and autumn, hurricanes sometimes hit the south and east coasts.

Warren Faidley

Lighting up the sky
This shot of lightning hitting storage tanks made Warren's name and meant he could be a full-time storm chaser. To take it he had to crawl past a nest of black widow spiders.

STORM CHASER'S CALENDAR

October
September
August
July
June
May
April

HURRICANES
THUNDERSTORMS
TORNADOES

THE WEATHER MACHINE

From the lightest shower to the wildest hurricane, our weather is created by three elements — water, air and heat from the Sun. The way they work together can be thought of as a kind of 'weather machine'. The Sun provides the warmth and light that make life on the Earth possible, and its energy powers the weather machine. When sunshine heats the oceans, sea water evaporates, turning into its gas form — water vapour — and becoming an invisible part of the air. And as the Sun warms the land and sea, this makes the air just above them become hotter too. As a result it rises upwards, cooling as it moves higher. This produces clouds, which in turn lead to storms.

HOT AND COLD

Hottest location
57.8°C
Al 'Aziziyah, Libya
13 September 1922

Hottest annual average
34.4°C
Dallol, Ethiopia
1960–66

Greatest 24-hour change
55.6°C (6.7°C to −49°C)
Browning, Montana, USA
23–24 January 1916

Coldest location
−89.2°C
Vostok Station, Antarctica
21 July 1983

The Earth is tilted

The Earth's path around the Sun

Sun

The heating effect of the Sun is strongest in the tropics, the belt north and south of the Equator. The Earth has a slight tilt, so that different parts of the planet are warmed more at different times of the year, causing the seasons.

Extremes of temperature
The Libyan desert is one of the hottest places on the Earth. In the tropics, the Sun is almost overhead throughout the year, which is why the heat is so intense. The Earth's coldest regions are towards the North and South poles. Tall mountain ranges are also icy, because the temperature is lower at this height in the atmosphere.

The Earth is surrounded by a layered blanket of air called the atmosphere. Most of our weather happens in the lowest part, which reaches up about as high as Mount Everest, but some storms are so powerful they punch through into the next level. Air is almost always moving from one place to another, and this is what we call wind. Some winds blow for immense distances across the Earth, while others may be confined to a single river valley. They occur because the Sun heats different parts of the planet's surface by different amounts, creating areas of warmer and cooler air. The winds drive the weather machine. They push the clouds, bringing rain, and when blocks of warm and cold air meet this produces weather systems that can generate dust storms and tornadoes.

Clear blue skies
The air is always pushing on us, even though we are not aware of it. This is called air pressure. When air sinks it creates an area of high pressure, which often brings clear skies with few clouds, as here in New Mexico, USA.

Grey and cloudy skies
Low pressure is often associated with sheets of cloud, as here in New Jersey, USA. When winds blow it is because air is moving from an area of higher pressure to an area of lower pressure – the air is trying to even itself out.

Cold air falls _____

Winds

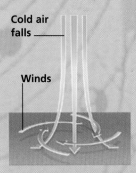

In an area of high pressure, cold air sinks downwards. Winds move out from the bottom.

Warm air rises

Winds

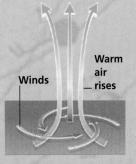

In an area of low pressure warm air rises up creating clouds and rain. Winds move inwards near ground level.

BEAUFORT SCALE (wind speed)

FORCE	EFFECT
0 (below 1km/h)	**Calm** air still; smoke rises straight up
1 (1–5km/h)	**Light air** flags do not move; rising smoke drifts
2 (6–11km/h)	**Light breeze** leaves rustle; smoke drifts in wind direction
3 (12–19km/h)	**Gentle breeze** leaves, twigs move; small flags flutter
4 (20–29km/h)	**Moderate breeze** small branches move; paper blows around
5 (30–38km/h)	**Fresh breeze** small trees sway; waves with crests form on lakes
6 (39–51km/h)	**Strong breeze** large branches sway; hard to use an umbrella
7 (51–61km/h)	**Near gale** whole trees sway; hard to walk against wind
8 (62–74km/h)	**Gale** twigs snap off trees; wind makes it difficult to walk
9 (75–86km/h)	**Strong gale** branches break; tiles, chimneys torn off roofs
10 (87–101km/h)	**Severe gale** trees snapped or uprooted by wind
11 (102–120km/h)	**Violent storm** trees blown around; cars overturned
12 (more than 120km/h)	**Hurricane** many trees torn up; buildings destroyed

Water covers nearly three-quarters of the Earth's surface. It is the fuel of the weather machine, and has an unusual and special quality. It can be found on this planet in its three forms – as solid ice, liquid water and water vapour gas – all at the same time. The amount of water on the planet always stays about the same, but it shifts between these three forms and moves to different places. In a process called the water cycle, water moves from the oceans to the air, where it exists as vapour and then as clouds, before falling as rain, snow or hail. Eventually, it rejoins the seas and the cycle begins again. Water's ability to change its form gives our climate its incredible variety. From spectacular flashes of lightning to the roaring descent of an avalanche, it also fuels the kinds of wild weather you will read about and explore in the rest of this book.

How rain is born
These tea pickers shelter from heavy rains in Darjeeling, India. As air rises and cools it can hold less and less water vapour. Clouds form when the vapour becomes tiny droplets of liquid water or, if the cloud is very high up, ice crystals. As droplets knock into each other they merge to make larger drops. These become too heavy to stay in the air and fall as rain. A raindrop is about 100 times the size of a cloud droplet.

WET AND DRY

Greatest 24-hour rainfall
1,870mm
Cilaos,
La Réunion, Indian Ocean
15–16 March 1952

Greatest annual rainfall
26,461mm
Cherrapunji,
Meghalaya, India
August 1860 to July 1861

Wettest location
11,872mm average
rainfall per year
Mawsynram,
Meghalaya, India

Driest location
0.5mm rainfall per year
Quillagua,
Atacama desert, Chile
1964–2001

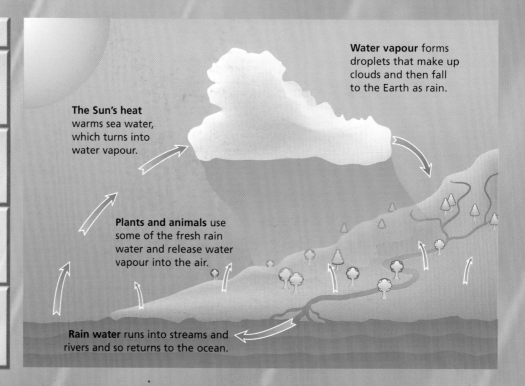

Water vapour forms droplets that make up clouds and then fall to the Earth as rain.

The Sun's heat warms sea water, which turns into water vapour.

Plants and animals use some of the fresh rain water and release water vapour into the air.

Rain water runs into streams and rivers and so returns to the ocean.

WATER

EXTREME CLOUDS

The wildest storm begins its life as a tiny, unremarkable cloud. If the conditions are right, a small cumulus cloud that is born on a summer morning will grow and grow through the heat of the day. It will reach upwards until it becomes a menacing tower that stretches from low in the sky to 10km above the ground – beyond the height that most aircraft fly. In the late afternoon or early evening, this fully grown, mature storm cloud may throw out streaks of lightning and balls of hail. As it rains, usually the cloud will lose its energy, break up and disappear. But sometimes a storm cloud will carry on shooting up through the atmosphere, bringing even more extreme weather, including tornadoes.

Flying saucers
When strong winds are forced up over a mountain range they can cause smooth disks of cloud, like these in Washington state, USA, to appear over the peaks. Called lenticular clouds, they look like a stack of plates – or a UFO (Unidentified Flying Object).

Thunder ahead
A towering cloud, such as this cumulonimbus incus in Colorado, USA, is the type that produces thunderstorms. It has a distinctive shape with a spreading top. This part of the cloud is called the anvil, or thunderhead. It forms when the cloud meets an invisible ceiling of warmer air.

Warning clouds
A domed cloud formation, called mammatus, looms over a church in Alberta, Canada. Mammatus hangs from beneath the anvil of a mature thunder cloud and is a sign of severe weather, especially tornadoes.

" *I've seen* storm clouds suddenly grow *to more than 15,000m,* topped with a spectacular circular anvil. *Any small cloud that tries to challenge these giants is sucked in and consumed for fuel. The shapes are amazing.* They look so solid you can imagine walking up the side *of them.* "

CLOUD FILE

Height	Cloud type	
Above 5,000m (16,500ft)	**Cirrus** **Wispy curls** of cirrus are the highest type of cloud.	
Above 5,000m (16,500ft)	**Cirrocumulus** **Tufted white** sheets like this are made of ice crystals.	
900–9,000m (3,000–30,000ft)	**Cumulonimbus** **Tall nimbus** clouds will bring showers of rain.	
600–1,950m (2,000–6,500ft)	**Stratocumulus** **Lumpy layers** of this cloud are common worldwide.	
600–1,200m (2,000–4,000ft)	**Cumulus** **Fluffy puffs** with a flat base are seen in summer.	
0–1,950m (0–6,500ft)	**Stratus** **Low sheets** of stratus stretch over hundreds of kilometres.	

THUNDERSTORMS

From the ancient Greeks to the Norse people, who lived in Scandinavia, many civilizations have believed in and made offerings to gods of thunder and lightning. Thunderstorms have always been one of nature's most powerful and awe-inspiring events. A single storm can release enough energy to supply the entire United States with electricity for 20 minutes. A flash of lightning is a huge electrical spark. Inside the upper part of a storm cloud, ice crystals form because the air is colder at this height. The crystals and water droplets are blown around violently and knock against each other. This creates electric charges — like rubbing a balloon against your hair. When the difference in charge is big enough, electricity leaps from one area to another, creating the lightning flash. We hear thunder because the lightning rapidly super-heats the air, making it explode.

High-rise strike
This photograph of the Eiffel Tower in Paris, France, taken in 1902, was one of the first ever to record lightning in a city. Tall buildings, mountains and radio and TV masts are often struck. The Empire State Building in New York City, USA, is hit about 100 times a year.

Lighting up the clouds
The electrical charges that build up in storm clouds can flow only when they are very large — which is why lightning is so bright. Bolts that jump from one cloud to another, or between parts of the same cloud, are called cloud-to-cloud lightning.

Ball lightning

This rare type of lightning can appear after a ground strike. Ball lightning is about the size of a beach ball, and may roll along or climb up objects before exploding or fading away. Scientists do not know its exact cause.

LIGHTNING FILE

Around the world: there are 1,800 storms going on at this moment

Stormiest place: Kampala, in Uganda, has storms on about 242 days a year

Width of a lightning bolt: a few centimetres

Length: up to 200km

Fulgurites: 'fossil lightning', produced when a strike melts the soil that it passes through.

" Lightning will seek out its target, attracted to even the smallest piece of metal, like a camera tripod or a zip. When you feel the hair on your arms stand on end, that's when you know it's getting close. You can sense the electrical energy building up. The antennas on my truck will sizzle and pop, too, and the radio starts to crackle. "

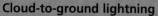

Cloud-to-ground lightning

There are 100 lightning strikes per second throughout the world, and about one bolt in four hits the earth. The electricity can travel under the ground, so you may be in danger even if you are some distance away.

Trails through the sky

In cloud-to-air lightning the charge leaps to the surrounding atmosphere. To tell how close a storm is, count the seconds between the flash and the thunder clap, then divide by three. This will tell you how far away it is in kilometres.

LIGHTNING STRIKES

Zigzag flashes of lightning cut across the sky. Trees, clouds and buildings are lit up for a split second with an eerie brightness. Lightning can be spectacular to watch, but it is also extremely dangerous. Around the world about 200 people a year are killed by lightning strikes. A single bolt carries enough electricity to power 150 million light bulbs, and heats the air it travels through to 30,000°C – five times the temperature of the Sun's surface. But there are also some amazing survival stories. A park ranger was hit seven times, and his worst injury was the loss of a toe.

WHAT HAPPENS WHEN LIGHTNING STRIKES

1 **Cats run for cover:** animals such as dogs and horses also become nervous before a storm

2 **Thunder cloud:** inside, there are strong currents of wind that blow up and down

3 **Raindrops:** can be huge, as the winds keep them up in the air until they are very heavy

4 **Chaser truck:** storm chasers have special equipment to track violent storms

5 **Hail:** during a thunderstorm, there are often showers of hailstones – balls of ice

6 **Cloud-to-ground lightning:** attracted to metal and will hit tall buildings and chimneys

7 **Cloud-to-air lightning:** will sometimes be seen even if the storm is too far away to hear

8 **Cloud-to-cloud lightning:** can light up the inside of a cloud so it glows like a giant lamp

9 **Fire hazard:** the heat from lightning can make trees explode and start wildfires

10 **Power cut:** lightning can cause a surge of electricity that knocks out power supplies

FLOODS

Water is vital for all life on Earth but it can also bring great destruction. Floods cause nearly half of all deaths from natural disasters around the world. Even in less severe floods people often have to be rescued from the roofs of their water-filled homes and farm animals may become stranded. If sewage gets into drinking water supplies, typhoid, cholera and other diseases can spread quickly. Most flooding is the result of heavy rainfall, although it can also be caused by melting snow or by the massive waves, called tsunami, that are triggered by undersea earthquakes. When large rivers overflow, huge areas may remain flooded for many weeks. In 1993, the Mississippi and Missouri rivers in the United States burst their banks at the same time, submerging more than 40,000km².

A region under water
Hurricanes and tropical storms often result in broadscale, or widespread, flooding. In 2004, rain from Tropical Storm Jeanne battered the city of Gonaives, in Haiti, for 30 hours. Floods and mudslides destroyed crops and homes, and many people lost their lives. Three-quarters of the city was covered by water and more than 250,000 people were left homeless.

Washed away
Rivers in flood can destroy homes, roads and bridges as well as cutting off services such as telephones and electricity. Here, the force of water washes away the soil beneath this house in the Italian Alps, until it collapses into the river below.

A flash flood

In December 1999, Cervinara, in
southern Italy, was hit by sudden
floods as extreme rainfall made
streams overflow in the hills around
the town. Flash floods occur when
huge amounts of rain fall during a
short period. Although they usually
affect only a small area, they are very
dangerous because people do not
have time to prepare. Flash floods
are more likely to occur where the
ground cannot absorb much water,
such as in rocky, mountainous
regions or in cities, where the soil
is covered by concrete and roads.

EL NIÑO

In 1997 and 1998, global weather was thrown into chaos. In Indonesia, vast forest fires raged after months of drought, filling the air with smoke so thick that drivers had to use headlights at midday. In Peru, there were severe floods, and a lake 145km long appeared in a desert that had been dry for 15 years. The cause was *El Niño* — a current of warm water that pushes through the Pacific Ocean towards South America every five to seven years. This has a dramatic effect on rainfall and temperatures around the world, from Africa to central Europe and Mongolia to the United States.

Storms in California, USA
The *El Niño* of 1997–98 fuelled huge waves along the coast of California, tornadoes in Florida and flooding in several US states. Winter temperatures were also higher.

The 1997 *El Niño* event is shown on this satellite image. The warm current moves east across the Pacific Ocean.

North America

South America

Warm *El Niño* current

Cool current

Pacific Ocean

Drought in Australia
This is the dried-up bed of Lake Burrendong. Droughts in Australia and Southeast Asia have been linked to *El Niño*, as it makes winds in the western Pacific drier than normal.

Floods in Brazil
Most of the city of Eldorado had to be evacuated after the local river broke its banks. In *El Niño* years, the warm, moist air brings unusually heavy rains, often causing flooding in South America.

STORMS

HURRICANE ALERT

As a hurricane approaches, you can hear the wind getting stronger. First comes the sound of rubbish being blown down the street and tiles falling from roofs. Then power lines begin to spark. Windows shatter and trees collapse to the ground as they are uprooted. The huge booms and crashes are the sound of buildings being ripped apart. Eventually, the wind is so loud that all you can hear is its whistling and roaring. These are the most powerful storms on the Earth. The largest contain hundreds of thunderstorms in circling bands, and measure up to 970km across. Even an average hurricane extends over an area twice the size of Ireland. Their devastating winds blow at the speed of a Formula One racing car, with some gusts reaching 300km/h.

The view from space
Satellite pictures, such as this one of Hurricane Andrew approaching Louisiana, USA, in 1992, allow scientists to track a hurricane as it develops. They look for groups of thunder clouds that are beginning to spin. Then, they watch to see if an 'eye' forms – the circular opening at the centre of the hurricane.

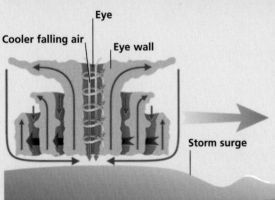

Eye

Cooler falling air

Eye wall

Storm surge

The strongest winds and storms are in the bank of cloud called the eye wall. Warm, moist air is drawn in at the bottom of the hurricane, and cooler air drops down the eye. Low pressure inside the eye makes the sea level rise, creating a storm surge. This can result in giant waves, which batter the coast.

Early warnings
Information from satellites, computers and radar allows forecasters to warn people where a hurricane is likely to strike. This has helped to save many lives.

Evacuation routes
In 1999, a 150km-long traffic jam snaked through South Carolina, USA, as residents of Charleston fled Hurricane Floyd by driving inland. Before evacuating their homes, people tried to limit hurricane damage by boarding up houses and businesses.

" The eye wall was upon us and I watched as the wind attacked a house. First, it got under the heavy storm shutters and started slamming them backwards and forwards. Seconds later, the windows vanished, and the rest of the house was slowly picked apart. "

Eyes in the sky
This US Navy aircraft is part of the Airborne Early Warning Squadron, which has tracked hurricanes since the 1940s. Some flights are made right into the eye, where there is no cloud and the wind is gentle. Flocks of birds are sometimes caught here and are unable to fly out during the storm.

SAFFIR-SIMPSON HURRICANE SCALE (wind speed)

CATEGORY	EFFECT
1 (118km/h–152km/h)	Slight damage. Trees and shrubs lose leaves and twigs. Storm surge flooding along coast roads.
2 (153km/h–176km/h)	Some trees blown over. Damage to mobile homes. Chimneys and tiles blown from roofs. Small boats may break from their moorings.
3 (177km/h–208km/h)	Leaves stripped off and large trees blown down. Mobile homes destroyed, small buildings damaged. Houses battered by floods.
4 (209km/h–248km/h)	Extreme damage to windows, roofs and doors. Mobile homes completely demolished. Floods up to 10km inland.
5 (more than 248km/h)	Catastrophic damage. Even strongly constructed buildings are affected. Small buildings blown away. Major flood damage.

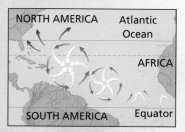

Hurricane
Direction of rotation
Path of hurricane

Hurricanes are born in the warm sea off the coast of Africa. The rotation of the Earth causes a cluster of thunder clouds to spin. This storm then moves northwest across the Atlantic Ocean, becoming stronger as it goes.

HURRICANE LANDFALL

Landfall – when a hurricane crosses on to the shore – is the time that everyone fears most. Towering waves pound the coast, rain pours down and ferocious winds blast through towns. The violent thunderstorms in the eye wall crackle with lightning, and some hurricanes even produce tornadoes. The result can be floods, mudslides and the destruction of entire neighbourhoods. In 1900, the whole city of Galveston in Texas, USA, was covered by water. In other parts of the world, hurricanes go by different names. In the northwest Pacific, which has the most severe storms, they are called typhoons. In the south Pacific and Indian Ocean they are known as cyclones. As a hurricane moves over land or cooler seas it begins to weaken as its 'fuel supply' of heat and moisture is cut off. But it has a sting in its tail, as the remaining clouds may still drop enough rain to cause serious flooding inland.

Atlantic hurricane damage
Atlantic hurricanes usually strike the Caribbean and southern USA, especially Florida, but sometimes their effects are felt further away. In 1987, this wood in Kent, England, was flattened when wind from the remains of a hurricane intensified a storm over southern Britain.

Hurricane Andrew
Arriving at 5am on a Sunday morning in August 1992, Andrew is one of only three Category 5 hurricanes to have hit the USA since records began. The five-metre storm surge ripped boats from their moorings, dragging some hundreds of metres inland. In just a few minutes, about 15,000 boats were destroyed

An expensive storm
This house in South Dade, Florida, USA, is one of more than 125,000 that were wrecked or destroyed by Hurricane Andrew. About 250,000 people lost their homes. It was the most costly natural disaster in US history, causing over US$25 billion worth of damage.

Path of destruction
The high winds in the eye wall of Hurricane Andrew cut a trail 40km wide. This Miami trailer park was turned into a field of rubble. But the worst damage from a hurricane is usually the result of flooding, caused by the storm surge and torrential rains.

TORNADO TOUCHDOWN

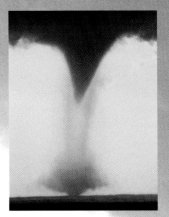

A funnel of whirling air begins to drop downwards from the wall cloud.

Tornadoes are the ultimate in wild weather. When the spiralling funnel of a tornado drops down from a storm cloud to touch the ground there is a boom that sounds like a huge explosion. The shape has been compared to a giant tail lashing across the landscape. A tornado can rip a house from its foundations, fling it through the air and leave it in pieces. This extreme type of storm, also known as a twister, is a column of powerful winds that spins at up to 500km/h, the speed of the world's fastest train. Tornadoes vary in strength, and can last from a few minutes to over an hour. The most violent twisters are in the United States, where about 1,000 are reported each year, but weaker ones occur on every continent apart from Antarctica. Britain, Russia, Australia and South Africa all experience large numbers of tornadoes. In Japan they are called 'dragon whirls'.

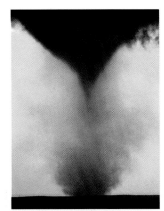

Low pressure inside the funnel creates a vacuum effect, sucking up dust.

" The strongest twister I've ever experienced was an F5. It looked like a giant smoke cloud rising high into the air. Branches were flying and trees bending right over until they almost touched the ground – and that was just from the winds on the outside of the tornado. I hit the brakes and turned around. My foot was shaking on the accelerator. "

Touchdown! The funnel reaches the ground to become a mature tornado.

Tornado storm cloud
This twister in Texas, USA, has descended from the wall cloud, which can be seen flaring out from the base of the storm. The storm cloud may extend to more than twice the height of Mount Everest. Tornadoes form when the rising air in a thunderstorm, called the updraft, begins to rotate.

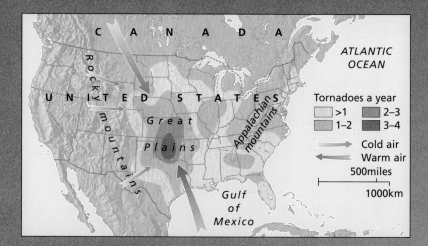

America's Great Plains are the world's tornado hot spot. With flat land stretching for many kilometres, and cold winds from Canada and the Rocky mountains clashing with warm, moist air from the Gulf of Mexico, the conditions in 'Tornado Alley' are ideal for twisters.

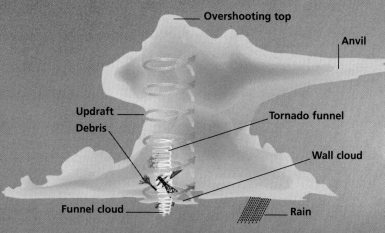

Tornadoes are produced by high-energy thunderstorms, especially a type called a supercell. When the conditions are right, warm air rushes up through the storm so powerfully that it bursts through the cloud ceiling, forming the overshooting top. This is one of the key signs that a tornado is on the way.

FUJITA SCALE
(wind speed)

FORCE	EFFECT
F0 (65km/h–115km/h)	Damages chimneys. Breaks branches off trees.
F1 (116km/h–180km/h)	Pulls tiles off roofs and overturns mobile homes. Pushes moving vehicles off the road.
F2 (181km/h–252km/h)	Bursts windows. Snaps or uproots large trees.
F3 (253km/h–331km/h)	Tears off roofs and pulls down walls of houses. Can overturn trains and uproot most of a forest.
F4 (332km/h–418km/h)	Flattens buildings. Throws cars through the air.
F5 (419km/h–511km/h)	Rips buildings from the ground. Flings vehicles more than 100m.

The damage caused by a tornado is used to measure its force. This scale was invented by the Japanese scientist Tetsuya Theodore Fujita.

PATH OF A TORNADO

In 1925, the Tri-State Tornado cut a terrible trail through Missouri, Illinois and Indiana in the United States, covering about 350km in four hours. This twister was so big it did not have a clearly defined funnel. Instead, witnesses said it resembled a dark fog rolling towards them. In general, the wider a tornado is, the stronger it is. The Tri-State measured 1.5km across at its base, although it may in fact have consisted of two or more funnels, merging in and out of one another. It was the deadliest twister in US history, destroying nine towns and causing nearly 700 deaths. However, tornadoes cause the most loss of life in Bangladesh, where a large number of people live in a small area. In the United States, there are far fewer victims now than in the past, mainly because today's networks of storm chasers and meteorologists – scientists who study the weather – can provide earlier warnings.

Twin twisters
These twin tornadoes near Dimmitt, Texas, are weak twisters called land spouts. Supercell storms will often give birth to more than one tornado, but usually the first dies out before the next one forms.

After touchdown the path of a tornado may be a straight line, zigzag or even a circle.

Destructive winds

This scene of devastation in Happy, Texas, was caused by a tornado in 2002. It also killed two people. The most costly tornado, around Oklahoma City in 1999, wrecked more than 2,000 homes and businesses, and resulted in US$1.2 billion worth of damage. Tornadoes cause the most destruction when they strike built-up areas. On average, Oklahoma City is struck by a damaging twister once every two years.

Flying cutlery

Tornadoes can snap trees and whip up debris that scrapes bark clean off. This fork was flung into the bare wood of a stump by winds of around 300km/h in Saragosa, Texas.

Wide-based tornado

This F3 twister near Laverne, Oklahoma, is about 400m wide. Other tornadoes look more like white strings of spaghetti. When a tornado has passed its peak intensity, it enters what is known as the rope stage. The funnel becomes thinner and leans over to one side. Finally, it dies away.

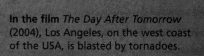

In the film *The Day After Tomorrow* (2004), Los Angeles, on the west coast of the USA, is blasted by tornadoes.

TWISTER

Tornadoes can have some very
unusual effects. Eyewitnesses have reported
herds of cattle lifted high above the ground, wells and
rivers sucked dry, and even a train torn from its tracks
and set down again, but facing in the opposite direction.
What happens inside a tornado is still something of a
mystery. However, in 1928, Will Keller, a farmer in Kansas,
USA, watched from his storm cellar as a funnel passed over.
He could see up into a circular opening that rose about 750m.
Smaller whirlwinds broke away around the edges of the funnel.

THE EFFECTS OF A TORNADO

1 **Sub-vortex:** a smaller funnel that may twist around main column

2 **Lightning:** often occurs with a tornado, sometimes seen flashing inside the funnel

3 **The funnel:** can be seen due to the cloud inside, and the dust and debris it has picked up

4 **Crops:** flattened by the spinning winds, which may make circular patterns similar to crop circles

5 **Wall cloud:** the part of the storm from which the tornado hangs down

6 **Path of destruction:** may crash into one house but leave another almost untouched, as the winds pass it by

7 **Spinning winds:** reaching 500km/h or more, these are what cause the most damage to homes

8 **Cattle:** huddle together and often do not move, even when twister is close. Sometimes they are lifted up

9 **Inside the tornado:** ripped-up plants, dust and soil, parts of houses and vehicles are whirled around

10 **A second tornado:** some storms give birth to more than one twister, but seeing two at once is rare

WAVES AND WATERSPOUTS

When the wind meets the sea it can create towering waves higher than a house. It can also form the twisting columns of cloud and spray known as waterspouts. Most waves are caused by the wind blowing against the surface of the sea. The size of a wave depends on how far it has travelled and the strength of the wind. Storm waves can reach more than 12m during a gale. The fierce winds of hurricanes, tornadoes and thunderstorms can sometimes force together groups of waves to make giant 'super-waves'. The biggest wave ever recorded was spotted in the Pacific in 1933. From its lowest point, called the trough, to its highest point, or crest, it measured 34m – higher than seven double-decker buses stacked on top of one another.

A famous storm
The film *The Perfect Storm* (2000) tells the story of the fishing boat *Andrea Gail*, which sank with all its crew in huge storm waves in October 1991. The storm raged along the east coast of North America, from the Caribbean to Canada. Many other crews were saved by the coast guards and navy helicopters.

The power of storm waves
Spray from a massive wave washes over the 30m-high Le Four lighthouse in Brittany, France. Storm waves can even pose a threat to oil rigs, and tip over large ships or smash them into pieces.

Storm surges

In 1965, Hurricane Betsy sent surf crashing into hotels lining Miami Beach in Florida, USA. As well as whipping up enormous waves, hurricanes cause the sea level beneath them to rise. The sea water sweeps over the coast and through towns and farms. The deadliest storm surges are in Bangladesh, in Asia.

" A bright flash of lightning lit up a huge wall of water *less than 30m away from where I was standing.* I had come face to face with a storm surge. *In the morning I saw the results – piles of dead fish, clothing and a ruined boat.* Even the palm trees had been turned into battered stumps *by the force of the water. "*

Multiple waterspouts

This line of waterspouts was seen off the coast of Albania. Waterspouts last for about 15 minutes and are usually too weak to cause much damage. However, in 1969 a swarm of six came ashore in Cyprus, in just a few hours, and killed four people.

Water whirlwinds

Waterspouts are columns of whirling air that occur over seas and lakes. They are usually narrower than tornadoes and reach up to about 500m – as high as the world's tallest building. Waterspouts may look as though they are made of spray, but the funnel actually contains water vapour from the air. Sometimes they suck up sea creatures such as fish, clams and jellyfish, which then fall inland as very strange rain.

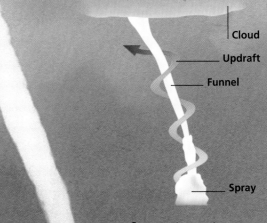

Cloud

Updraft

Funnel

Spray

Some waterspouts are tornadoes over water, but most do not need severe storms to form. Air above a warm sea, such as in tropical areas, rises rapidly to create an updraft. Rotating air currents near the sea surface cause the updraft to spin. The low pressure inside the funnel sucks up spray at the bottom, while the top links to a cloud.

DUST STORMS

In deserts and other dry areas, winds may whip up storms of sand and dust so vast they can be seen from space. Sometimes the hot conditions also produce whirlwinds of super-heated air called dust devils. As a dust storm approaches, birds sound warning cries and animals such as camels bellow with alarm. In the distance the storm looks like a solid bank of cloud rising from the ground. It arrives as a wave of tumbling, choking dust. The cloud can be 1,500m tall, almost four times the height of the Empire State Building in New York City. The grains of dust may drift for thousands of kilometres, high up in the atmosphere. Sand from the Sahara desert in Africa falls as far away as northern Europe and the Amazon in South America.

*" The winds around a dust devil are strong enough to knock you over, **but once you are inside it is strangely still.** It is as hot as an oven in there, and **as the Sun filters through** the spinning wall of desert grit, **it creates this weird orange glow.** Up above, tumbleweeds and dust dance around but beyond them the funnel opens up into blue sky. "*

Dust storms form when warm winds meet a wall of cooler air, called a cold front. Air rushes in to replace the rising warm air, making swirling clouds of dust and sand.

Dust cloud

Warm air

Cold front

The Dust Bowl
A dust storm looms over homes in Texas, USA, in 1935. During the 1930s, dust storms devastated an area from Kansas to New Mexico, which became known as the Dust Bowl. Many farmers and their families had to leave because soil was blown away, destroying farmland.

Braving the sand
Children battle a dust storm in Xiahe, China. Sand blows across the country from the Taklimakan desert in the northeast and the Gobi desert to the north. Dust storms are common in deserts but they also form in other regions where the soil has become dry and dusty. This can happen when there is a long drought and where there are few plants to hold the soil together.

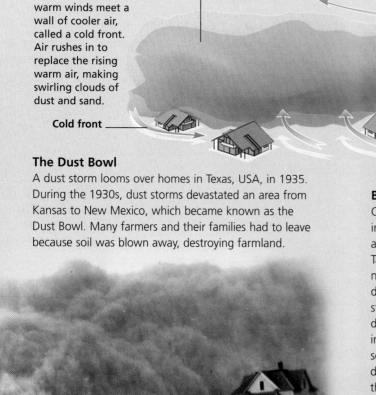

Red sky in the city

A dust cloud engulfs Beijing in China, turning day into night. Drivers cannot see properly, so traffic moves slowly, and airports have to be closed. As the dust passes over cities and factories it picks up pollution, which will spread to wherever the dust takes it.

Desert whirlwinds

Dust devils, like this one in Tucson, Arizona, USA, are spinning funnels of air that are visible because of the dust, twigs and other debris they pick up. These small whirlwinds do not usually cause much damage, but some are powerful enough to turn over a car. Dust devils are formed in deserts and other places where the ground is hot and the conditions are dry. They can range in height from just a few metres to about a kilometre.

Wind

Dust and debris

Funnel

Heated ground

Dust devils form when the Sun beats down on open land, strongly heating the air above the ground so that it rises as an updraft. A section of air may then begin to rotate because it is whipped around by winds blowing in the area.

SOLAR WINDS

It is not only the Earth that has wild weather. On the Sun, storms produced by sunspots – the dark patches on the surface – throw bursts of particles out into space. These form part of the solar wind that 'blows' from the Sun all through our galaxy. A million tonnes of particles per second stream towards our planet and produce auroras hundreds of kilometres above the surface of the Earth. These stunning light displays appear in different forms, including bands of light, bright arches and rippling curtains of reds, blues and greens. You usually need to be close to the Arctic or Antarctic Circle to see them. The Inuit people of Labrador, in northeast Canada, believed they were torches carried by spirits to show them the way to heaven.

Aurora Australis
The green glow of the *Aurora Australis* over Antarctica was photographed from the Space Shuttle. When the Sun's storms are at their peak, which happens every 11 years, the *Aurora Borealis* may be seen on Earth as far south as Athens, Greece, and the *Aurora Australis* as far north as Brisbane, Australia.

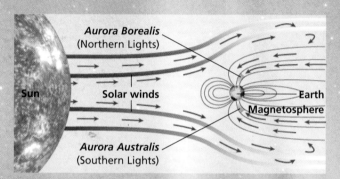

Aurora Borealis (Northern Lights)

Sun

Solar winds

Earth Magnetosphere

Aurora Australis (Southern Lights)

The Earth is surrounded by an invisible envelope of magnetic force, called the magnetosphere. The part of the magnetosphere facing the Sun is rounded, while the other side forms a tail like that of a comet. Particles from the solar wind get into the magnetosphere through the tail and are carried towards the poles. When they crash into gases in the Earth's atmosphere light is released, creating the auroras.

Aurora Borealis
Also known as the Northern Lights, here the *Aurora Borealis* illuminates the sky in Finland. In the southern hemisphere, this effect is called the *Aurora Australis*, or Southern Lights.

FIRE AND ICE

EXTREME HEAT

The highest temperature ever recorded was near the coast of Libya in North Africa. In September 1922, it reached a searing 57.8°C. Deserts, which occur where the annual rainfall is less than 25cm, experience some of the most extreme heat on the planet. The most dramatic changes of temperature within a day also happen here. During daylight hours, the clear skies mean that the Sun constantly beats down. After dark there is no protective blanket of cloud to conserve the warmth, so the temperature can suddenly drop, sometimes to freezing. But hot, dry weather is found from the Mediterranean to Australia. And during a heat wave, even countries with normally mild climates are exposed to days or weeks of scorching sunshine.

Rainforest humidity
In the rainforests that are found towards the Equator, such as this one in Costa Rica, it is both hot and wet. The temperature rarely goes above 34°C, but the humidity level – the amount of water vapour in the air – is high. These areas may receive 6,500mm of rain a year, ten times as much as in London, Paris or San Francisco.

Drought in the Sahel
At this refugee camp in Darfur, Sudan, people are queuing at the only well. Millions of people had to leave their villages because of war, but extreme weather also played a part. Darfur is in the Sahel, a dry area south of the Sahara that is kept from becoming desert only by the seasonal rains. These failed for many years, making it difficult for any crops to grow.

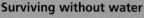

Surviving without water
Catfish are able to survive even when rivers and lakes have been reduced to puddles. Some catfish can breathe through their skin instead of their gills, and bury themselves in the mud. Others wriggle across land for short distances to find a pool containing more water.

DROUGHT

It begins when the expected rains fail. Plants start to wilt, then shrivel up. Trees drop their leaves to prevent losing water through them. The soil is baked as hard as concrete, or turns to dust that is blown away by the wind. In tinder-dry forests, wildfires may blaze out of control. Reservoirs empty and rivers become a trickle or disappear, while livestock, such as cattle and sheep, struggle to find enough to eat. A severe drought can have a devastating impact on local wildlife, farming and people, and its effects can last for many years. A drought happens when less rain than normal falls over a period of several weeks or longer. This can occur anywhere, including Sudan, the United States, Australia and even the Amazon rainforest.

Animals become ill

A prolonged drought has weakened these cattle, belonging to the Samburu herders of Kenya. Grazing areas and water are hard to find so animals are more likely to become ill or to die from hunger.

DROUGHT RELIEF

The effects of drought are most devastating in regions that are already hot and dry. About one billion people around the world live in this kind of environment, where water is in short supply and the soil is only just good enough to farm. If the rainfall is lower than usual it tips the balance. As crops fail and animals become sick, a famine can follow. Many people may starve as a result unless they receive help. Eventually, the weather pattern changes. Even the 30-year drought in the Sahel area of Africa came to an end in the 1980s. Today, scientists are finding ways to predict changes in rainfall patterns, which are linked to the movement of ocean currents such as *El Niño*. In the future, they may be able to forecast when and where droughts are likely to happen so that people have more time to prepare.

Watering hole
This herd of African buffalo is drinking from a pool refilled by rain. Drought can destroy the habitats where wild birds, fish and animals live. As a result, endangered species are more likely to become extinct, but many creatures survive by migrating to less affected areas.

Desert bloom
These flowers in the Mojave desert, California, USA, spring up after the winter rains. They complete their whole life cycle – from shoot to flower to seed – in the few weeks before the summer heat. The hardy seeds then wait until the next shower.

Replanting the forests
Since 1977, the Green Belt Movement has been involved in planting 30 million trees in Kenya and other African countries. Deforestation, where trees are cut down for farming or timber, makes soil more likely to turn to dust. The new trees will help to reduce the effects of drought.

A water source
Villagers flock to this well in Gujarat, India, because the reservoirs, wells and ponds in neighbouring areas have dried up. During a drought, people may have to travel great distances to fetch water, or wait hours for tankers to arrive with supplies of fresh water from other parts of the country.

Imaginary lake
This pool in the Australian outback is a mirage – an optical illusion usually seen over deserts or other flat, treeless areas. When the air near to the ground gets very hot, it bends light so that objects above the horizon appear to be below it. Because the sky is blue, the mirage looks like the shimmering water of a lake.

Relief from the heat
A spray of water created by a broken pipe keeps these children cool during a heat wave. Periods of unusually high temperatures can be deadly. In 2003, a heatwave across Europe killed 27,000 people.

The earth dries up
The Atacama desert in Chile is the driest place on our planet. Showers pass over only a few times a century, and the average yearly rainfall is less than a millimetre. When there is no rain, reservoirs and riverbeds like this one dry up.

Crops die out
The plants that are naturally found in drier regions have adapted so that they can live with little rain or re-grow quickly after drought. But crops such as this maize need enough water to produce the fruits and seeds we eat. In a drought, the harvest will be smaller, or crops may die completely.

Breaking the drought

The arrival of rain brings welcome relief for these villagers in Somalia. Some droughts end slowly, as rainfall gradually returns to normal. Others are broken with a sudden torrential downpour. Where the soil is baked hard this can bring its own problems, such as flooding.

A relief camp

Famine drives large numbers of people away from their homelands as they seek out desperately needed food, water and medicine. Many, like these children, find shelter and a meal in relief camps.

International aid

The Red Cross, the United Nations and governments and charities worldwide send emergency food relief to areas where there is famine. After the drought has ended, people begin to rebuild their lives, digging wells to provide water and planting new crops.

WILDFIRES

Each year, tens of thousands of wildfires begin around the world. Some are small and burn themselves out, while others billow into vast walls of flame that blacken hillsides and turn buildings into scorched ruins. In the United States, a total area of 17,000 km² – almost as large as Israel – burns in an average year. These fires are most common in California, Australia and the south of France, where the type of plants and weather conditions make it easy for wildfires to take hold. Sweet-smelling trees and bushes, such as eucalyptus, are filled with oils that act like fire-lighters, while the hot Sun and droughts dry out plants and timber. Warm winds then fan the flames and drive the fire onwards at speeds up to 25km/h.

City in danger
A fire in the Catalina hills around Tucson, Arizona, USA, heads towards the city. About half of all wildfires are sparked by lightning. Many others are started deliberately or caused by human carelessness, including cigarettes and camp fires that have not been put out properly.

Fiery weather
Clouds called pyrocumulus sometimes form as the hot air from a wildfire rises, taking moisture with it. These clouds may also bring lightning, which can start more fires. The smoke from wildfires drifts high up into the atmosphere, turning sunsets deep orange and red.

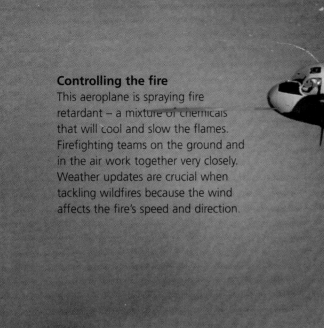

Controlling the fire
This aeroplane is spraying fire
retardant – a mixture of chemicals
that will cool and slow the flames.
Firefighting teams on the ground and
in the air work together very closely.
Weather updates are crucial when
tackling wildfires because the wind
affects the fire's speed and direction.

Quick-spreading fires
Some fires burn along the ground but others,
called crown fires, leap from the top of one
tree to the next. Gusts of wind may send hot
embers into the air and so start new blazes.
Ferocious fires can even create spinning
funnels of wind, called fire whirls, that hurl
burning logs through the air.

OUT OF THE FLAMES

Wildfires are destructive and deadly, but they are also a natural process. Some trees only release their seeds after burning, or need fires to clear away other plants so that their seedlings can reach the light. In the forests of California, USA, fires are a vital part of the giant redwood tree's life cycle. Wildfires clear decayed logs and diseased plants, while ash makes soil more fertile. The result is that new growth can flourish in place of old.

WHAT HAPPENS IN A WILDFIRE

1 **Fire-fighting helicopter:** carries a container that can drop hundreds of litres of water on to the flames below

2 **Far hillside:** even trees many kilometres away are not safe if the wind blows in this direction

3 **Firefighters:** may use hoses on smaller fires and build firebreaks to stop larger blazes spreading

4 **Smoke:** will stream out as it is blown by the wind, showing where the fire will move next

5 **Bare hill:** with no protective plants, heavy rains can lead to flooding and mudslides

6 **Burnt-out building:** many homes are so badly damaged they cannot be repaired. Often people move away

7 **Blooming again:** some plants, such as this catspaw, flower better after fire

8 **Charred tree:** thick bark can give protection from the flames

Fire-proof seeds

This seed pod, from an Australian bush called banksia, looks as though it has been burned up. But it can survive fire even if the plant itself has been killed. In fact, the heat makes the seed cases open up, and new banksias grow as soon as it rains.

SNOW

A deep, muffled 'thunk' is the sound that marks the beginning of the deadliest type of avalanche. It is the noise of hundreds of thousands of tonnes of snow cracking away from the mountainside and shattering like a huge pane of glass. In a blizzard, snowflakes are whipped into an icy storm, but avalanches are snowy weather at its most extreme. As the snow sheet roars downhill, it gathers up deadly ice chunks and rocks. It can also generate high-speed winds that snap trees and rip roofs from houses. When the avalanche stops, the debris sets like concrete in a few seconds, making it impossible to dig your way out without help. Those who have survived the impact of an avalanche are very lucky – only one in 20 victims is rescued alive.

Crystal stars
Snowflakes grow into different shapes depending on the weather conditions high in the clouds where they form.

Snow storm
Snowploughs cleared the streets of New York after it was brought to a standstill by one of the worst blizzards in the city's history, in 2003. Blizzards occur when strong winds and heavy snow combine.

Life in the Antarctic
These emperor penguins can survive colder temperatures than any other animal. A layer of fat and thick, downy feathers protect them from icy winds that blow at up to 200km/h.

How avalanches form

Loose powder avalanches, such as this one in Antarctica, occur when light snow cascades off a mountain. They usually start from a single point and get wider as they fall further. Slab avalanches are much more dangerous. A massive plate of snow breaks free and thunders down at speeds of 100km/h or more. If a slope is good for skiing, then it is at risk of an avalanche.

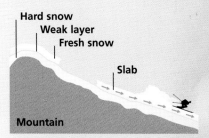

Hard snow
Weak layer
Fresh snow
Slab
Mountain

A slab avalanche forms when a heavy fall of new snow, or existing snow blown by the wind, piles up quickly on top of a weak layer. The weight causes the weak layer of snow to crack and slide downwards.

Avalanche rescue

These rescuers are using long poles, called probes, to find exactly where a victim is buried. Sniffer dogs and the radio signals from devices called beacons can also help to locate people.

Destruction in Galtür

It took only 50 seconds for a huge wall of snow and rubble, 100m high and weighing 300,000 tonnes, to smash through this Austrian village in 1999, killing 31 people.

Ice storm
A strong, cold wind has driven drops of freezing rain on to one side of this tree in Switzerland. During the ice storm they blew along the surface and then froze solid.

ICE

Much of the Earth's water is locked up as ice. In winter, the ice sheets that cover the land and oceans at the North and South poles spread over more than 30 million square kilometres in total – an area so big it would blot out all of Africa. Extreme cold can be fatal for humans, but icy weather is destructive in other ways too. Icebergs can sink ships – the most famous, the *Titanic*, was lost in the North Atlantic with 1,517 passengers and crew in 1912. In an ice storm, lashing rain freezes to form a glaze of ice that can be as much as 20cm thick. Roads become dangerously slippery and power supplies fail as cables break under the weight. Hail can also be deadly. In 1986, hailstones, many weighing more than a kilogram, killed 92 people in Bangladesh.

Iceberg islands
These icebergs near Antarctica are shearing off an ice shelf, a thick sheet of ice covering the sea. Nine-tenths of an iceberg lies under water, which is why they are a danger to ships. The largest ever recorded was half the size of Wales.

Balls of ice
Hailstones form in thunder clouds. A tiny ice crystal is coated with layer upon layer of ice as it is blown around inside the cloud. When the hailstone becomes too heavy for the updraft – the wind that blows upwards – to keep it in the air, it falls to the ground. The largest ever reported were said to be the size of pumpkins.

Building with ice
Each year, the *Icehotel* in Kiruna, Lapland, is rebuilt using 3,000 tonnes of ice and vast amounts of snow. The idea was inspired by the igloos of the Inuit people, made from snow carved into blocks.

*" Hail can be from pea-sized to grapefruit-sized or more. I've had **hail the size of tennis balls hit the truck** and leave large dents. It is probably **the scariest thing a storm chaser runs into.** Imagine driving down the street and people throwing fist-sized rocks. "*

Frozen waterfalls
When a waterfall freezes, it provides a challenging vertical sheet of ice for climbers. During winters with a long cold spell, even Niagara Falls on the US-Canadian border will freeze over. At more than 1km wide, they are the world's second largest falls. The river does not stop flowing, but the falling water can make ice mounds 15m thick. A bridge of ice can also form, extending for several kilometres to link the two banks.

GLOSSARY

Air pressure the pressure exerted by the atmosphere, measured as the weight of air pressing on a given area.

Anvil the flat top of a thunder cloud, which resembles the heavy steel block used by blacksmiths.

Atmosphere the blanket of gases that extends nearly 800km above the Earth.

Auroras the Northern Lights and Southern Lights, caused by the solar wind.

Avalanche a mass of loose snow or a huge snow slab moving rapidly down a slope.

Beaufort scale a scale from 0 to 12 that classifies the strength of a wind by its effects on the landscape.

Blizzard a combination of heavy snow and high winds producing severe weather.

Broadscale flooding floods across a wide area, when heavy rain over a long period saturates the soil and makes rivers overflow.

Cirrus strands of cloud that form above 5,000m and are blown into streaks.

Climate the general weather conditions in a region over a long period.

Cold front the front edge of a mass of cold air.

Cumulonimbus a cumulus cloud that produces heavy rain, hail and thunderstorms.

Cumulus tall, puffy clouds that form when 'parcels' of warmed air rise and cool.

Cyclone 1. the name for a hurricane in the south Pacific or Indian Ocean; 2. a rotating low pressure system.

Desert an area with almost no vegetation and little rain.

Drought when less rain than normal falls in a region for an extended time.

Dust Bowl, the the Great Plains and Midwest of the USA in the 1930s, when heat waves, drought and over-farming caused dust storms.

Dust devil a column of spinning air and dust.

Dust storm a vast moving cloud of dust that reduces visibility to 1km or less.

El Niño a warm current in the Pacific Ocean that affects global weather patterns.

Electric charge a property of all particles. When large charges build up in clouds they can cause lightning.

Equator the imaginary line around the middle of the Earth that divides the northern hemisphere from the southern hemisphere.

Evaporation when liquid water turns to water vapour.

Eye the calm, often cloud-free centre of a hurricane.

Eye wall the ring of storm clouds around the eye.

Flash flooding a sudden flood, usually as a result of intense rain in a small area.

Fujita scale a scale from F0 to F5 that rates the strength of tornadoes based on the damage they have caused.

Funnel a cone or column of spinning air, as in a tornado or dust devil.

Funnel cloud the cloud inside a tornado funnel, formed because low pressure makes the water vapour in the air become droplets.

Gale a strong wind blowing at about 50km/h or more.

High pressure when air is sinking down in an area. It often brings clear skies.

Hurricane an intense storm born in the tropics with winds of 119km/h or more.

Ice storm a storm of freezing cold rain that sets to a solid glaze of ice when it hits the ground or objects.

Landfall when a hurricane crosses from sea on to land.

Low pressure when air is rising up in an area.

Magnetosphere the region of space, like an invisible envelope around the planet, where the Earth's magnetic field has an effect.

Mammatus clumps of cloud that hang from the anvil of a thunder cloud. *Mamma* is Latin for breast.

Meteorologist a person who studies the science of weather.

Mirage an optical illusion often seen in deserts, usually taking the form of a pool of shimmering water.

Mudslide when water-soaked soil turns to mud and slides down a slope.

Ocean current a movement of water, like a river in the ocean, often caused by winds.

Overshooting top a dome rising above the anvil of a thunder cloud, caused by extremely strong updrafts.

Storm chaser someone who tracks, and travels in search of, severe storms.

Storm surge the rise in sea level caused by an area of low pressure and by its winds. Hurricanes create the most extreme storm surges.

Stratus the lowest type of cloud, formed when a large amount of warm, moist air rises gently.

Sub-vortex a smaller funnel inside or around the main funnel of a tornado. Plural: sub-vortices.

Thunder cloud a powerful cumulonimbus cloud that produces lightning.

Tornado a violently rotating column of wind, which extends from a storm cloud and touches the ground.

Tropical storm a storm that begins in the tropics. A very strong tropical storm is called a hurricane, cyclone or typhoon, depending on its location.

Tropics the region north and south of the Equator, between the Tropic of Cancer and the Tropic of Capricorn.

Tsunami a massive wave caused by an earthquake on the ocean floor.

Typhoon the name for a hurricane in the northwest Pacific Ocean.

Updraft an air current that moves vertically upwards.

Wall cloud a portion of cloud at the bottom of a storm, from which tornadoes may descend.

Water cycle the constant movement of water between the oceans, air and land.

Water vapour water in its gas form.

Waterspout a funnel of spinning wind over water.

Wildfire an uncontrolled fire in forests, bush or grassland. Known in Australia as a bushfire.

Pyrocumulus cumulus clouds that are formed when moist air is made to rise by the heat of a wildfire.

Saffir-Simpson scale a scale from Category 1 to Category 5 used to rate the strength of hurricanes.

Solar wind a stream of particles from the Sun.

INDEX

Publisher: Sue Grabham
Editor: Clive Wilson
Additional editorial: Simon Holland
Senior designer: Carol Ann Davis
Additional design:
  Heidi Appleton, Mike Davis,
  and Malcolm Parchment
Picture research manager:
  Cee Weston-Baker
DTP manager: Nicky Studdart
Production manager:
  Nancy Roberts
Indexer and proofreader:
  Sheila Clewley
Consultant: Wayne Elliott,
  Met Office
Additional research:
  Carol Ann Davis

KINGFISHER

Kingfisher Publications Plc
New Penderel House
283–288 High Holborn
London WC1V 7HZ
www.kingfisherpub.com

First published by
Kingfisher Publications Plc 2006

1TR/0705/TWP/CLSN(CLSN)/150ENSO/F

10 9 8 7 6 5 4 3 2 1

Printed in Singapore

Copyright © Kingfisher
Publications Plc 2005

ISBN-13: 978-0-7534-1184-1
ISBN-10: 0-7534-1184-9

ACKNOWLEDGEMENTS

The publisher would like to thank the following for permission to reproduce their material. Every care has been taken to trace copyright holders. However, if there have been unintentional omissions or failure to trace copyright holders, we apologize and will, if informed, endeavour to make corrections in any future edition.

Key: *b* = bottom, *c* = centre, *l* = left, *r* = right, *t* = top

Cover Warren Faidley/Photolibrary.com; back cover *l* Corbis/William James Warren; back cover *r* Science Photo Library/Kenneth Libbrecht (SPL); pages 1 Corbis Kevin R. Morris; 2*tl* Warren Faidley; 2*cl* Associated Press; 2–3*b* Photolibrary.com/ Warren Faidley; 3*tl* Warren Faidley; 3*r* Warren Faidley; 4 SPL/Susan McCartney; 4*b* Corbis/Sergio Pitamitz; 5*c* Getty Photographer's Choice; 5*b* Getty Photographer's Choice; 6 Corbis/Reuters; 7 Alamy/Steve Bloom; 8–9 Getty Stone; 8*bl* Rex Features; 9*tl* Photolibrary.com; 9*tr* Warren Faidley; 9*tcr* Warren Faidley; 9*cr* Corbis/Paul Souders; 9*cr* SPL/Pascal Goetgheluck; 9*br* Warren Faidley; 9*br* Alamy; 10*l* National Oceanic and Atmospheric Administration, USA; 10*br* Getty; 11*bl* Warren Faidley; 11*tr* SPL/Peter Menzel; 11*bl* Corbis/Jim Reed; 12–13 Corbis/Tim Davis; Warren Faidley; Photolibrary.com; Getty Stone; 14*tr* Rex Features; 14 Associated Press; 14–15*b* Rex Features; 16*t* Warren Faidley; 16*c* Corbis/Sygma; 16*b* Photolibrary.com; 17 Getty Imagebank; 18*cl* National Oceanic and Atmospheric Administration, USA; 19*tl* Corbis/Reuters; 19*tc* Corbis/Sygma; 18–19*c* Corbis/Bettmann; 20*tr* Getty Stone; 20 Warren Faidley; 21*t* Photolibrary.com; 21*b* Corbis/Roger Ball; 22–23 Warren Faidley; 24 Warren Faidley; 25*tr* Warren Faidley; 25*c* Warren Faidley; 25*cr* Warren Faidley; 25*br* Kobal; 26–27 Getty Imagebank; Getty Taxi; Corbis/Peter Beck; Corbis/Kevin R. Morris; Warren Faidley; 28*l* Corbis/Jean Gulchard; 28*cr* Corbis/Sygma; 29*tl* Rex Features; 29*bl* Frank Lane Picture Agency; 30*bl* National Oceanic and Atmospheric Administration, USA; Corbis/Michael Yamashita; 31*t* Corbis/Lio Lingun; 31*r* Warren Faidley; 32 SPL/Pekka Parviainen; 32*tr* Corbis; 34–35 Still Pictures; 34*tl* Photolibrary.com; 34*bl* Photolibrary.com; 35*t* Photolibrary.com; 35*br* Corbis/Bettmann; 36*l* Corbis/Adrian Arbib; 37*bl* Corbis/Wendy Stone; 37*tr* Corbis/Peter Johnson; 37*cr* Corbis; 38–39 Corbis/Reuters; 40 Corbis/David Turnley; 40 Corbis/Viviane Moos; 40*b* Corbis/Chris Rainier; 41 Photolibrary.com; 41*br* Corbis/Richard Hamilton Smith; 42–43 Getty Stone; 42*tr* Alamy/A.T. Willett; 42*cl* Corbis; 43*tr* Corbis/ Vince Streano; 44–45 Photolibrary.com; Getty News; ANT Photolibrary, Australia; Still Pictures; 46*tr* SPL; 46*cr* Alamy/Richard Levine; 46*b* Frank Lane Picture Agency; 47*t* Still Pictures; 47*bl* Corbis/Reuters; 47*br* Corbis/Sygma; 48*tl* Rex Features; 48*cl* SPL/Jim Reed; 48*b* Frank Lane Picture Agency; 49*tl* Getty Robert Harding Picture Library; 49*r* Photolibrary.com; 50–51 Photolibrary.com; 52–53 Corbis/Paul Souder; 54 Photolibrary.com

The publisher would like to thank the following illustrators:
4–5 Jurgen Ziewe (Lightning strikes); 26–27 Peter Bull (Twister); 44–45 Mike Davis (Out of the flames); 4–5, 6, 18–19, 23, 29, 30–31, 32 Peter Winfield (weather artworks)